GROWTH IN AMERICA: 1865-1914

GLORY TO GOD IN THE HIGHEST. ON EARTH PEACE. GOOD WILL TOWARD

LIBERTY AND UNION NOW AND FOR EVER

North American Historical Atlases

GROWTH IN AMERICA: 1865-1914

Rebecca Stefoff

BENCHMARK BOOKS

MARSHALL CAVENDISH
NEW YORK

Benchmark Books
Marshall Cavendish
99 White Plains Road
Tarrytown, New York 10591

• • •

Library of Congress Cataloging-in-Publication Data
Stefoff, Rebecca, 1951–
Growth in America: 1865–1914/by Rebecca Stefoff
p. cm—(North American historical atlases)
Includes bibliographical references and index.
Summary: Discusses the recovery and development of the United States after the devastation
of the Civil War, with attention to the discovery of gold in the West, the building of the Transcontinental
Railroad, the surge of immigration, and America's emergence as a world power in the twentieth century.
ISBN 0-7614-1349-9 (lib.bdg.)
1. United States—History—1865–1921—Juvenile literature.   2. United States—History—1865–1921—Maps—Juvenile literature.
3. United States—Economic conditions—1865–1918—Juvenile literature.   [1. United States—History—1865–1921.]   I. Title.
E661 S825   2003   2002006206   973.8—dc21

• • •

Printed in Hong Kong
1 3 5 7 8 6 4 2

• • •

Book Designer: Judith Turziano
Photo Researcher: Candlepants Incorporated

• • •

Contents

Chapter One

AMERICA'S NEW ECONOMY

The Civil War nearly tore the United States apart in the early 1860s. And as the wounds of war slowly healed, the United States changed. The North had won the Civil War partly because of its superiority in manufacturing industries and railroads. Now those things were increasingly important to the whole nation. People started to work, communicate, and travel in new ways. Founded as a nation of farmers, the United States was becoming an industrial power.

Gold and Silver!

The discovery of gold in a northern California stream in 1848 sparked a gold rush as thousands of hopeful prospectors hurried to the region. The California gold rush was just the beginning. Prospectors who failed to find gold in California—and most of them did fail—roamed the West, hoping to strike it rich. Another rush in the Rocky Mountains of Colorado began in 1858 after a few miners found gold around Pikes Peak. More than fifty thousand people swarmed to the area, crying, "Pikes Peak or Bust!" Unfortunately, most of those who made it to Pikes Peak *did* wind up busted. Very few prospectors ever made their fortunes—or even a decent living—from gold mining.

Other gold strikes followed in Idaho, Montana, and Wyoming. In South Dakota, prospectors flocked to the Black Hills. The

A miner works deep underground in Nevada's Comstock Mine during the 1860s. Discovered in 1859, the Comstock contained some gold and much silver. The huge mining operation shaped Nevada's economy for twenty years.

United States government had given that area to the Indians in a treaty, but after the discovery of gold, the Indians were forced to give up their rights to the area. Sometimes, when looking for gold, prospectors struck silver instead. Although silver was less valuable than gold, great wealth was made from silver mines in

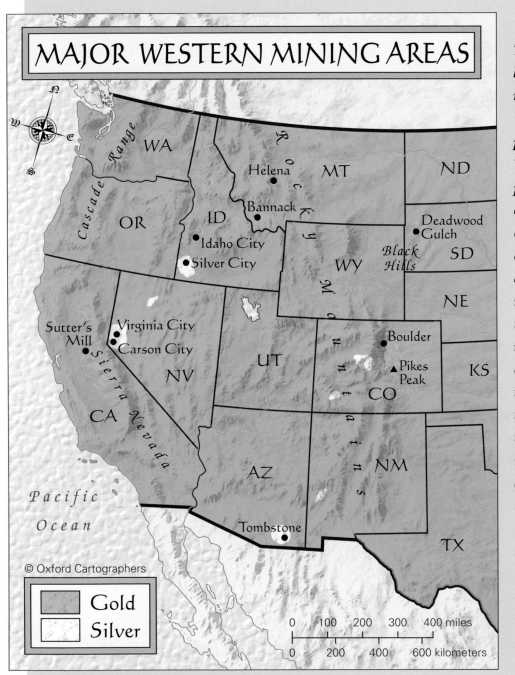

MAJOR WESTERN MINING AREAS

Cascade Range

WA

Helena

MT

ND

Rocky

OR

ID

Bannack

Idaho City

Silver City

Deadwood Gulch

Black Hills

SD

WY

NE

Sutter's Mill

Virginia City

Carson City

NV

Sierra Nevada

UT

Boulder

Pikes Peak

CO

KS

CA

Mountains

AZ

NM

Pacific Ocean

Tombstone

TX

© Oxford Cartographers

Gold

Silver

0   100   200   300   400 miles

0   200   400   600 kilometers

The news that gold or silver had been discovered in some remote and wild part of the West was enough to bring people rushing to the spot. The first to arrive were prospectors, who worked alone or in small groups. Then came merchants, shopkeepers, entertainers, physicians, and others to meet the miners' needs. Before long, the biggest claims passed into the hands of organized companies, and the prospectors became employees. Once the mines had been emptied of their precious metals, the mining towns often fell into decay as people left to seek their fortunes elsewhere. Sometimes, however, people stayed on to farm, ranch, or practice their trades, and the towns remained and grew. In this way, the gold and silver rushes helped to populate the West.

Nevada, Idaho, Colorado, and Arizona.

There were two types of mining in the West. One involved individual or small groups of prospectors. They looked for gold near the surface of the land. Sometimes they sifted specks of it from rivers or streams, and sometimes they scraped it out of the earth. The other type of mining required machinery. Most of the

BOOMTOWNS AND GHOST TOWNS

 Wherever miners found gold or silver, a camp of tents or shacks sprang up almost overnight. Soon, if the strike proved big enough, wooden buildings rose and a town took shape. These mining communities were called boomtowns because they grew explosively fast. In Nevada, mining began in 1859, following the discovery of a rich silver deposit known as the Comstock Lode. Less than two years later, Virginia City materialized nearby, complete with an opera house and more than a hundred saloons. For a short time, Virginia City was the second-largest city in the West, after San Francisco. But when the silver mines ran dry, the city's population dropped from 30,000 to about 4,000 in a few years. Before long, Virginia City was abandoned. Many boomtowns were entirely deserted when people left to seek their fortunes elsewhere. Left to wind, rain, and tumbleweeds, they became ghost towns, slowly crumbling into the landscape. Nevada alone has about 700 ghost towns.

At its peak in the 1860s, Virginia City had many businesses, including this office of the Wells Fargo & Company Express, which carried mail and freight across the West.

gold and silver lay in lodes or veins far below the surface, mixed with rock. Getting at these precious metals required digging shafts and tunnels, bringing chunks of **ore** to the surface, and melting or crushing the ore to release the metal. Such tasks were far beyond the lone miner. Companies, not solitary prospectors, did most of the mining in the West. They also reaped most of the rewards.

Across the Continent

During the first half of the nineteenth century, people from the eastern part of the United States settled in the Pacific territories of Oregon and California. The Great Plains and the Rocky Mountains were set aside for the Native Americans—many people thought that these territories were too dry and barren to be useful. But before long, some Americans began to think that the Plains could support cattle ranching, perhaps even farming. The U.S. Congress passed laws that opened the region to settlers and moved the Indians to smaller territories called **reservations**. One of these laws was the Homestead Act of 1862, which gave settlers land if they built homes on it and worked it. The Homestead Act encouraged thousands of families and individuals, including many single women, to settle on the Plains. Roads and towns began to appear in the nation's vast middle section, knitting together the country's Atlantic and Pacific coasts.

A photograph from the 1890s captures two of the forces that changed communication and travel in America during the second half of the nineteenth century. The telegraph pole on the right is one of hundreds of thousands strung across the landscape, holding wires to carry instant messages. Below it, a railroad track snakes through a canyon.

The coasts of the United States were being connected in other ways as well. In the 1840s, inventor Samuel Morse had shown that people could communicate almost instantly over long distances using his telegraph, a device that sent coded signals along wires. Stringing telegraph

During the second half of the nineteenth century, Americans got used to seeing maps that highlighted the way the western part of their country was being tamed, settled, and developed. This 1867 map shows mail routes in the West, "compiled from the latest information." The routes match the patterns of those followed by railway and road networks.

THE MOST FAMOUS MAIL SERVICE IN THE WORLD

The telegraph doomed a famous mail-carrying service in the West. Starting in April 1860, Pony Express riders carried bags of mail between San Francisco, California, and Saint Joseph, Missouri. Every ten miles or so, the riders got fresh horses at special stations set up for this very purpose. Riders covered seventy or eighty miles a day before turning over their bags to fresh riders. The Pony Express could cover the 2,000 miles between San Francisco and Saint Joseph in ten days, much faster than the mail companies that used wagons and stagecoaches. The riders, mostly teenage boys and young men, were cheered as heroes for riding through storms and Indian attacks. But even they could not outrace the new technology. The Pony Express ended in October 1861, two days after the first telegraph message passed between San Francisco and Washington, D.C.

Although the Pony Express ran for less than two years, its riders became the subject of tales and legends. Tough, brave, and resourceful, they had qualities that Americans liked to see in themselves and their nation.

wires on poles from city to city in the East was a challenge, but doing it across the enormous empty expanses of the West proved to be an ordeal. By October 1861, however, the work was done. News that once took more than a week to travel from one coast to the other could now flash across the continent in an instant.

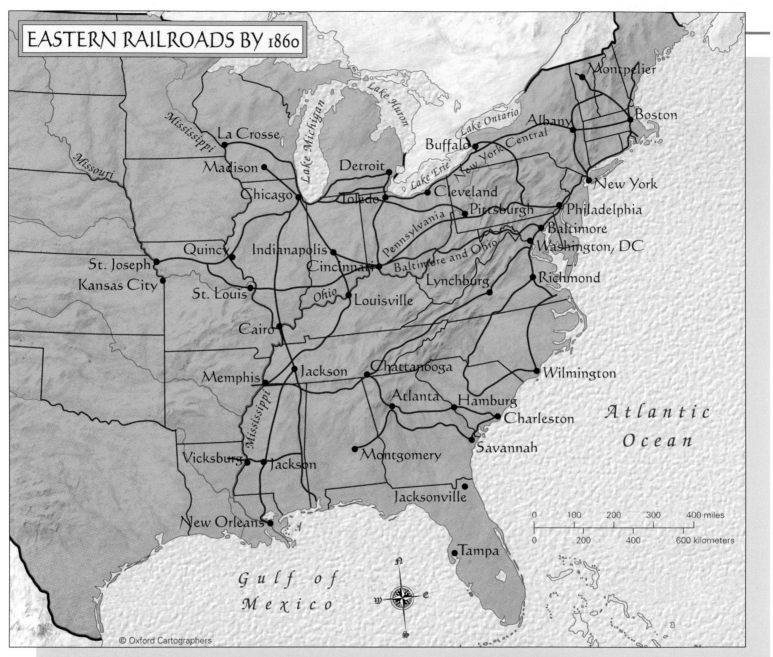

EASTERN RAILROADS BY 1860

Montpelier

Boston

Albany

Buffalo

New York Central

New York

Lake Ontario

Lake Erie

Detroit

Cleveland

Pittsburgh

Philadelphia

Toledo

Pennsylvania

Baltimore

Washington, DC

Lake Michigan

Lake Huron

La Crosse

Madison

Chicago

Mississippi

Missouri

Quincy

Indianapolis

Cincinnati

Baltimore and Ohio

Lynchburg

Richmond

St. Joseph

Kansas City

St. Louis

Ohio

Louisville

Cairo

Memphis

Jackson

Chattanooga

Wilmington

Atlanta

Hamburg

Charleston

Mississippi

Savannah

Vicksburg

Jackson

Montgomery

Atlantic Ocean

Jacksonville

New Orleans

Tampa

Gulf of Mexico

| 0 | 100 | 200 | 300 | 400 miles |
| 0 | 200 | 400 | | 600 kilometers |

© Oxford Cartographers

The first steam-powered train operated in Great Britain in 1829. Soon Americans developed steam trains of their own, and by 1840, the United States had 3,000 miles of railways. Twenty years later, that number had increased tenfold. About 30,000 miles of track, mostly in the East, linked mines, factories, and agricultural centers to cities and ports.

The Race of the Iron Horses

The telegraph was fine for sending news and messages to the West, but what about people and goods? Railroads were the answer. By 1860, a network of tracks connected many points in the eastern United States, especially in the North. Building a railway across the West was the next step, and it was so important that Congress took time in 1862—in the middle of the Civil War—to order the work to begin.

Two railway companies raced to complete the job. The Union Pacific Railroad Company started in Omaha, Nebraska, which was already connected to the eastern network, and laid track westward. The Central Pacific laid track eastward from Sacramento, California. The plan was for them to meet. Each company wanted to lay more track than the other

On May 10, 1869, a ceremony at Promontory Point, Utah, marked the meeting of the tracks that formed the first railway line across the entire United States. The New York Daily Tribune *reported, "The Post-Office Department has received a telegram from Promontory Point, stating that the mails have been delivered at that place to the Central Pacific [Railroad], and that the through line has been regularly established." From that time on, mail, freight, and passengers could travel by train from the East Coast to San Francisco in days instead of weeks.*

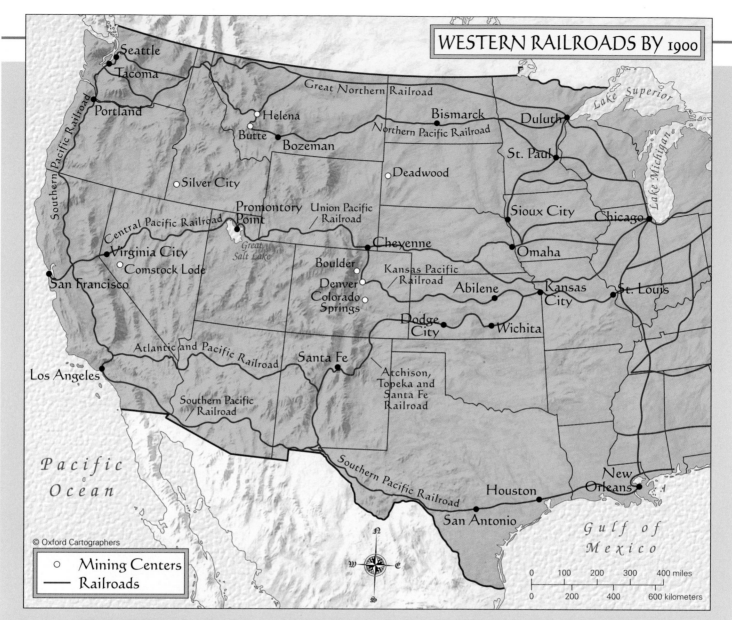

Seattle
Tacoma
Portland
Southern Pacific Railroad
Helena
Butte
Bozeman
Silver City
Great Northern Railroad
Bismarck
Northern Pacific Railroad
Duluth
Lake Superior
St. Paul
Deadwood
Promontory Point
Central Pacific Railroad
Great Salt Lake
Union Pacific Railroad
Sioux City
Chicago
Lake Michigan
Virginia City
Comstock Lode
Cheyenne
Boulder
Denver
Colorado Springs
Kansas Pacific Railroad
Omaha
Abilene
Kansas City
St. Louis
San Francisco
Atlantic and Pacific Railroad
Dodge City
Wichita
Los Angeles
Santa Fe
Atchison, Topeka and Santa Fe Railroad
Southern Pacific Railroad
Pacific Ocean
Southern Pacific Railroad
Houston
San Antonio
New Orleans
Gulf of Mexico

© Oxford Cartographers

○ Mining Centers
— Railroads

N
W   E
S

| 0 | 100 | 200 | 300 | 400 miles |
| 0 | 200 | 400 | | 600 kilometers |

The building of railroads across the West was a one of the great industrial success stories of the late nineteenth century. Thousands of people—including many Chinese and Irish immigrants—labored to lay track. They blasted tunnels through mountains, built bridges across gorges, and endured extremes of heat and cold. As a result, by the end of the century, several railways spanned the continent, and the United States had some 193,000 miles of railways.

Growth in America: 1865–1914

because Congress awarded land and money for each mile laid. Both faced difficulties. The Union Pacific had to haul timber from hundreds of miles away to lay track on the treeless

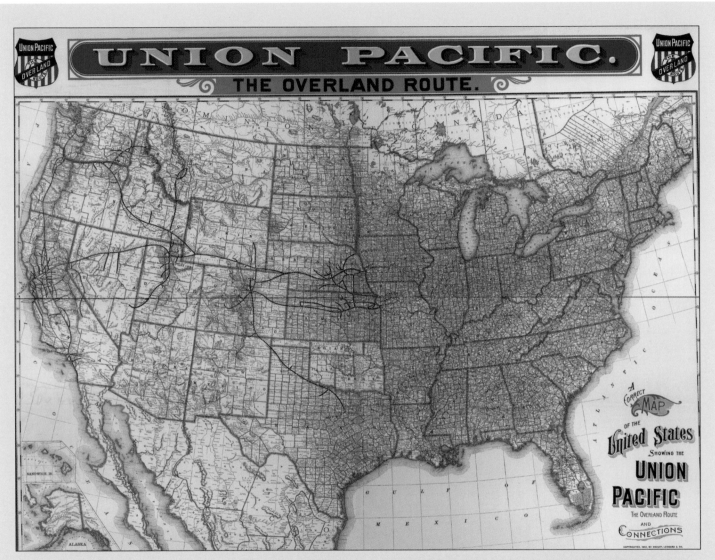

Nineteenth-century railroad companies gave out maps celebrating their routes. This map was made by the Union Pacific company, which built part of the first transcontinental railway line. The "Overland Route" had once been the Oregon Trail, used by wagon trains. Now the term was used for the new railway lines across the West. The right-hand side of the map appears much darker than the left-hand side because counties are smaller and towns are much more numerous in the eastern United States than in the West.

Plains. The Central Pacific had to bridge deep canyons in the Sierra Nevada and then cross the bleak desert of Nevada. The tremendous engineering feat was completed when the two tracks joined at Promontory Point in northern Utah in 1869.

The railroad revolutionized transportation. People and materials crossed the country in days instead of weeks. Trains created a truly **transcontinental** economy, hauling raw materials such as timber and ore to factories, moving grain to ports and cattle to markets, and shipping manufactured goods to communities that had once been isolated. Soon a web of railways covered the West, and new towns grew up along them.

Inventions and Industry

The late nineteenth century was a golden age of invention in America. Engineers, machinists, and tinkerers created hundreds of thousands of

Henry Ford's Model T gave ordinary Americans the freedom of the open road.
It also gave a boost to a number of industries, including road construction,
rubber manufacturing (for tires), and oil refining (for gasoline).

The Wright brothers' glider plane. Like many other inventors, the Wrights experimented with gliders, which do not have engines, before tackling the problem of developing an engine-powered airplane—a problem they solved in 1903. It did not take long for their success to transform transportation. In 1914, the world's first scheduled commercial airline service began operating in the United States. It was a single plane that carried freight and passengers along a twenty-two-mile route between Tampa and St. Petersburg, Florida. Within a few more years, much of the country would be served by regular mail and passenger flights.

inventions. Some of these inventions changed life in the United States and around the world. Among the most important and far-reaching of these inventions were Alexander Graham Bell's telephone (1876), Thomas Alva Edison's record player (1877), the incandescent electric light bulb (1879), and electric power stations (the first one opened in 1882), and George Eastman's small, easy-to-use Kodak camera (1888).

Inventors in both Europe and the United States experimented with new forms of transportation. A number of them developed "horseless carriages" driven by gasoline motors. The first automobiles were costly novelties, but in 1908, American engineer Henry Ford introduced his Model T, an affordable car designed for the common person. Americans loved it—some 15 million Model Ts were sold in nineteen

Garment workers in New York City in 1908. Thousands of people, many of them immigrants, toiled in clothing factories called sweatshops, which were generally unhealthy and unsafe. Some of the sweatshop workers became reformers who fought for laws requiring better wages and conditions.

years. Inventors also took to the air. Many of them worked on building an engine-powered aircraft, but Wilbur and Orville Wright made the first successful flight in 1903. Mail and passenger flights soon followed.

The railroad companies were the first business giants of the nineteenth century. Oil companies were another. The oil industry was born when it was discovered that petroleum, a black oil that oozed from the ground, produced light and heat when burned. Soon people were drilling for oil in many parts of the country, and in 1870, John D. Rockefeller formed Standard Oil, a company that eventually controlled most of the country's oil wells and **refineries**. Around the same time, Andrew Carnegie formed a company that gained control of nearly a quarter of the country's iron and steel production. The rise of big corporations like the oil and steel companies propelled the United States into an age of industrial achievement, but it also created problems. Workers' wages stayed low, while wealth and power were concentrated in the hands of a few "captains of industry." In 1890, Congress took a step toward limiting the power of big corporations by passing the Sherman Antitrust Act, a law designed to keep companies or individuals from controlling whole industries. The act was a victory for the Progressive Movement, whose reformers worked to improve the working and living conditions of laborers.

Chapter Two

IMMIGRATION AND URBAN GROWTH

The first European settlers in North America were **immigrants**, people who left their homelands for life in a different country. The late nineteenth century brought a new wave of immigration that broadened the definition of what it meant to be an American. **Immigration** also shaped another trend of the times: the growth of cities, as the United States began changing from a **rural** nation to an **urban** one.

Jewish immigrants pray in New York City in 1905. Jews were among the waves of many newcomers who began arriving in the United States in the 1880s, bringing new energy and broadening American culture. But not everyone welcomed the nation's growing diversity. Some Americans felt fear and hostility toward people of different ethnic or religious backgrounds.

New Arrivals from Europe

From its earliest days, America had been home to Africans, Jews, Roman Catholics, and people from many, many nations. But the great majority of Americans were white Protestants from England, Scotland, Germany, and other countries in northern and western Europe. Immigrants from those countries as well as Ireland and Sweden kept coming to the United States throughout the nineteenth century, and many of them homesteaded on the Plains. Another group of immigrants, made up of Greeks, Russians, Poles, Czechs, Italians, and other people from southern and eastern Europe, began arriving in the United States in the later years of the nineteenth century. By 1900, about 300,000 of these so-called "new" immigrants were arriving each year, compared with about 100,000 from northern and western Europe. Their arrival alarmed some native-born Americans, who feared that the newcomers would take jobs away from "real" Americans and would weaken America's traditional identity.

Many of the new immigrants were Catholics or Jews, and many spoke no English. They had come to America in search of work, and they almost always found jobs—although most received low wages. Finding it hard to fit into American society, immigrants tended to settle together in ethnic neighborhoods in New York, Chicago, and other fast-growing cities.

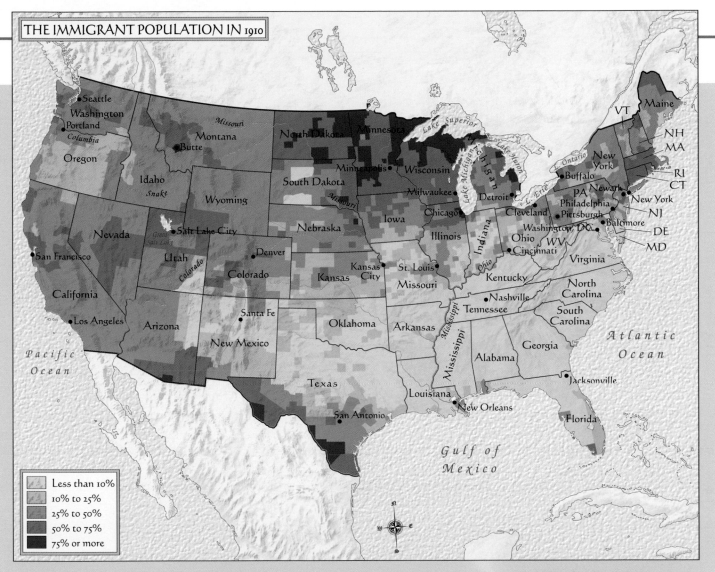

Seattle
Washington
Portland
Columbia
Oregon

Missouri
Montana
•Butte

North Dakota
Minnesota
Lake Superior

VT
Maine

NH
MA

Idaho
Snake

Wyoming

South Dakota
Missouri

Minneapolis•
Wisconsin
Milwaukee•

Michigan

New York
Buffalo•

RI
CT

Nevada

Great Salt Lake
•Salt Lake City

Nebraska

Iowa
Chicago•

Lake Michigan
L. Erie
Detroit

L. Ontario
PA
Newark•
Philadelphia•
Cleveland•
Pittsburgh•

New York

NJ

San Francisco•

Utah
•Denver
Colorado

Illinois

Indiana
Ohio
Cincinnati•

Washington, DC•
Ohio
WV

Baltimore•

DE
MD

California

Colorado

Kansas
City•
St. Louis•

Kentucky

Virginia

•Los Angeles

Arizona

Santa Fe•

Kansas

Missouri

Nashville•
Tennessee

North
Carolina

*Pacific
Ocean*

New Mexico

Oklahoma

Arkansas

Mississippi

South
Carolina

Georgia

*Atlantic
Ocean*

Texas

Louisiana

Alabama

Jacksonville•

Mississippi

Florida

San Antonio•

New Orleans•

*Gulf of
Mexico*

Less than 10%
10% to 25%
25% to 50%
50% to 75%
75% or more

*This map shows the result of the immigration wave that swept across the United States
in the late nineteenth century. The darker shades are regions where the 1910 population
contained many people who had been born in other countries, or who had at least one foreign-
born parent. Lighter shades mean a lower percentage of immigrants. The South had fewer
immigrants than other parts of the country, because it lacked two things that immigrants
wanted: land and industrial jobs. By the 1880s, most southern land was already owned, and
little was available for newcomers. The South also lagged behind the Northeast in industry.
Immigrants were concentrated in Boston, New York, Chicago, and the other great industrial
centers of the Northeast and Midwest. They also went to areas where land was available
for homesteading, such as Minnesota and the Great Plains, and to places where they could
work as miners, shepherds, or farm laborers, such as Nevada, Utah, and California.*

They and their children struggled to find the right balance between keeping their native languages and cultures alive and assimilating, or blending, into the English-speaking culture of their new home.

Asian Americans

Most immigrants from Europe arrived on the East Coast of the United States, but the West Coast also received new arrivals. Immigrants from Asia began landing on California's shores in the 1850s. The first to arrive were Chinese men who came to work in the gold mines of the Sierra Nevada and on railroad crews. Most planned to earn some money and return to China within a few years. Although some did

Japanese immigrants in the West often found work in agricultural areas. Their labor, along with the skillful farming techniques they introduced, helped make California's Central Valley into an important center of fruit and vegetable production.

THE OTHER IMMIGRANT ISLAND

 Starting in the late nineteenth century, immigrants from Europe were greeted in New York Harbor by the Statue of Liberty. They then entered the country at a government-run station on Ellis Island, where an immigration museum now stands. But on the other side of the continent, another island offered the first glimpse of America for many who came from Asia. Immigrants arriving in San Francisco passed through a station on Angel Island in San Francisco Bay. They often spent several weeks there, waiting for the authorities to approve their entry papers. During this anxious time, some carved their names or short poems on the walls. One Chinese immigrant wrote: "Imprisoned in the wooden building day after day, My freedom withheld: How can I bear to talk about it?"

return to their homeland, many remained in the United States and sent for wives and family members to join them. They founded the first Asian-American urban communities, such as San Francisco's Chinatown, and they also ran stores, laundries, and other businesses in small towns across the West.

Japanese immigrants began arriving in sizeable numbers in the 1880s. Many became farmers in California's fertile Central Valley. Koreans, Filipinos, and East Indians came a little later, in the early years of the twentieth century. They encountered racial prejudice from some white Americans. At times they also struggled against laws that limited Asian immigration and prevented Asians from owning land. But the immigrants and their children endured these hardships and remained, weaving threads of Asian heritage into the fabric of American life.

The Growth of the Cities

Most immigrants in the eastern and midwestern parts of the United States settled in urban environments. Many found work in the steel factories of Pittsburgh or the meat-processing plants of Chicago. In the sweatshops of New York City, immigrant women and girls labored long hours stitching mass-marketed clothing. The flow of immigrants enlarged America's cities and made them more diverse. By 1890, more than three-quarters of the population of many eastern and midwestern cities—including New York,

The fast-growing cities of the United States had traffic jams even before cars were common. A photograph taken in 1909 at the corner of Dearborn and Randolph Streets in Chicago reveals a mass of streetcars, wagons, and pedestrians choking the intersection.

Chicago, and Detroit—was made up of immigrants and the children of immigrants.

Native-born Americans also migrated to the cities in the late nineteenth century. Fewer people were needed for farm work, now eased by new equipment such as steel plows and milking machines. Freed from labor, many young men and women left the farm to look for jobs and excitement in the cities. In the South, large numbers of African Americans also fled the racism and poverty of the countryside, hoping that cities such as Montgomery and Atlanta would offer work and the chance of a better life.

One result of increased immigration was the rapid rise in the populations of cities. But urban growth was also fed by Americans migrating from the countryside to the towns. By the end of the nineteenth century, the United States was on its way to becoming a primarily urban nation. In the East, Boston, New York City, Philadelphia, Baltimore, Chicago, and St. Louis each had more than half a million people, and smaller cities were growing fast. Western cities such as San Francisco, Los Angeles, and Seattle would soon become major population centers, as well.

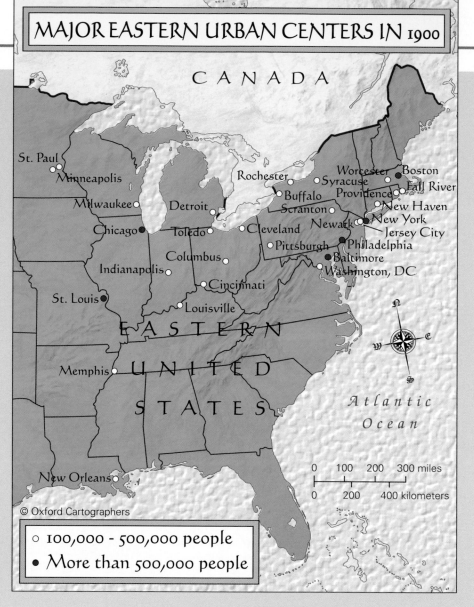

MAJOR EASTERN URBAN CENTERS IN 1900

CANADA

EASTERN UNITED STATES

Atlantic Ocean

© Oxford Cartographers

○ 100,000 - 500,000 people
● More than 500,000 people

Immigration and movement within the country started a major and lasting change in the nature of the United States. From the beginning of American history, the rural population had outnumbered the urban population. By 1860, on the eve of the Civil War, the United States had about 26 million people living in the country and about 8 million in cities or towns. But as the nation's total population grew during the rest of the century, the balance shifted. The urban population grew faster than the rural population. By 1900, about 43 million people

New York landlords turned buildings into tenements, which had many small apartments, often without much air or sunlight. Crowding and the lack of clean water made many tenements unhealthy, but these dwellings were also settings for the shops and the social life around which immigrant communities revolved.

lived in the country, compared with 30 million in cities and towns. The urban population still lagged behind the rural population, but it was catching up fast.

A Changing Landscape

The American landscape changed dramatically during the second half of the nineteenth century. Some of the changes reflected the simple fact of population growth. The country had more people, so of course it needed bigger

cities and towns and more villages, roads, and railroads. Other changes had to do with new ways of living and working.

As land grew scarce in the cities, architects began designing taller buildings that used new inventions, such as iron and steel beams and passenger elevators. In 1885, the first skyscraper, ten stories tall, rose in Chicago. Before long, Americans were getting used to the sight of even taller buildings in major cities. As early as 1859, author Mark Twain had complained that New York was so big that it took a whole day to get anywhere. By the end of the century, motorized

Chicago in 1890, when the city's skyline had already begun to change as buildings became taller. Soon cities would grow skyward with amazing speed, as skyscrapers sprouted in all big cities.

Cities grew not only up (with the building of skyscrapers), but also out, as farmland on their outskirts was covered with houses, factories, and shops. As immigration swelled New York City's population, the demand for housing spread onto nearby Long Island. In 1908, a real-estate development company made this map to promote property it was selling in Brooklyn, a part of New York City that is located on Long Island. The company was selling lots in the red squares in the "Empire Keystone Improvement" district of Brooklyn. According to the map, some of the land to the north was still covered with fields and trees.

streetcars and underground trains called subways were beginning to make urban travel faster and easier. And now that so many people lived in cities and never even saw the countryside, city planners began setting aside land for public parks, places for outdoor recreation. These developments set the pattern for urban growth and planning throughout the twentieth century. At the same time, industrial growth also introduced less appealing new features to the urban landscape, including smog, pollution, and the slums that housed low-paid factory workers.

America's rural landscape was changing, too, especially in the Great Plains. Homesteaders set-

Created by an act of the U.S. Congress in 1872, Yellowstone was the world's first national park, an area set aside to be owned and enjoyed by all citizens because of its natural splendors, which include amazing hot springs and geysers, deep canyons, and forests. After the Union Pacific Railroad built a line to the area, the company issued maps and photographs to draw visitors to the park. These materials gave many Americans their first glimpses of the glories of their western landscape.

tled more and more of that region. Their steel plows bit through the dense native grasses, turning prairies into fields. Windmills dotted the land, powering the pumps that drew underground water into the dry fields, and countless miles of a new invention, barbed wire, marked property lines. Oklahoma, once known as Indian Territory, was the last part of the Plains that was opened to settlement. In 1889, a flood of homesteaders streamed across its borders in a land rush that marked the end of the western frontier. By the end of the century, almost all of the western territories had become states, and the West was no longer very wild.

Chapter Three

BECOMING A WORLD POWER

YOUR
COUNTRY
CALLS YOU

R·M·WRIG '98

While the United States experienced many internal changes during the late nineteenth century, the nation also began looking beyond its own borders and taking a growing role in international affairs. Seeking trade relations with the rest of the world, the United States sometimes flexed its military muscles to force other nations such as Japan to open their ports to U.S. merchants. In addition, Americans had grown used to moving into new frontiers as their country expanded westward. Once the nation spanned North America, where would it find a new frontier? The country that had begun as a colony of the British empire started to want colonies of its own, just like such European countries as France and Germany. By 1887, the hundredth anniversary of the signing of the U.S. Constitution, America was becoming a world power.

Adding Alaska

The United States acquired its first new frontier even before it had finished settling the old one. In 1867, Secretary of State William H.

In the late 1890s, hopeful prospectors clustered at Dyea Flats on the coast of southeastern Alaska, preparing to scale mountain passes and raft down turbulent rivers on their way to the gold fields of Canada's Yukon Territory and inland Alaska. American writer Hamlin Garland joined this gold rush and called it "the last march of that kind which could ever come to America, so rapidly were the wild spaces being filled up."

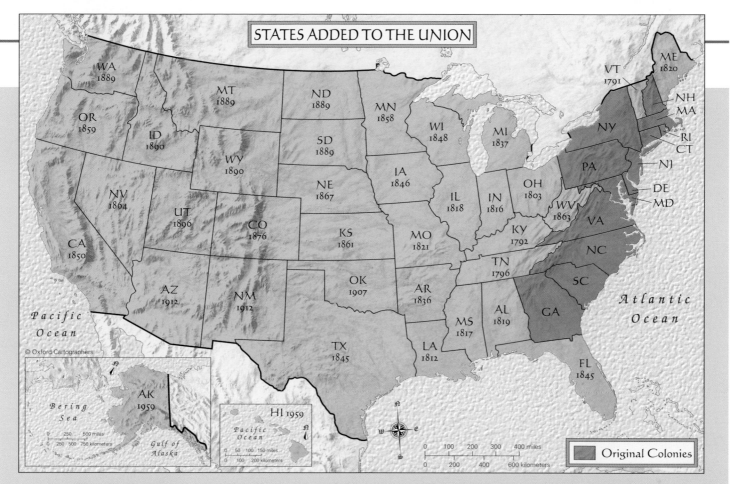

STATES ADDED TO THE UNION

WA 1889
OR 1859
ID 1890
MT 1889
ND 1889
MN 1858
WI 1848
MI 1837
VT 1791
ME 1820
NH
MA
NY
RI
CT
NJ
PA
DE
MD
WV 1863
VA
SD 1889
WY 1890
NE 1867
IA 1846
IL 1818
IN 1816
OH 1803
NV 1864
UT 1896
CO 1876
KS 1861
MO 1821
KY 1792
NC
CA 1850
AZ 1912
NM 1912
OK 1907
AR 1836
TN 1796
SC
Pacific Ocean
GA
TX 1845
MS 1817
AL 1819
LA 1812
FL 1845
Atlantic Ocean
© Oxford Cartographers
AK 1959
Bering Sea
Gulf of Alaska
HI 1959
Pacific Ocean
Original Colonies

The United States originally consisted of thirteen former British colonies. The first new states were added to the union in the 1790s, not long after the country gained its independence. In the years that followed, the United States continued to gain territory on its western frontier. These wild and unsettled western territories became populated and organized, and one by one they became new states. The second half of the nineteenth century saw the creation of many states in the West. The last western territories to achieve statehood were Arizona and New Mexico, the forty-seventh and forty-eighth states, in 1912.

Seward arranged for the United States to buy Alaska from Russia, which had claimed Alaska years earlier and established a small colony there. The $7.2 million purchase price seemed steep to most Americans, who grumbled about paying for Seward's "polar bear garden."

When prospectors found gold in Alaska in the 1890s, Americans changed their tune

EXPLORING AMERICA'S NEW NORTHLAND

 Even before the United States purchased Alaska, Americans were exploring it. Western Union, the largest telegraph company in the United States, wanted to run telegraph wires across Canada and Alaska and then across the Bering Sea to Russia. The company sent teams of surveyors and scientists north to search for a good route for the lines. In early 1867, though, Western Union called off the mission. The first intercontinental telegraph line had just been laid across the bed of the Atlantic Ocean, connecting North America and Europe, and the line to Russia was no longer needed. But one surveyor, William Healey Dall, had fallen in love with Alaska. He decided to stay and study the land and its inhabitants and wildlife. Soon the purchase of Alaska made Americans curious about the place, and Dall was just the man to satisfy their curiosity. In 1870, he published *Alaska and Its Resources*, a book that made him the country's leading expert on its new territory.

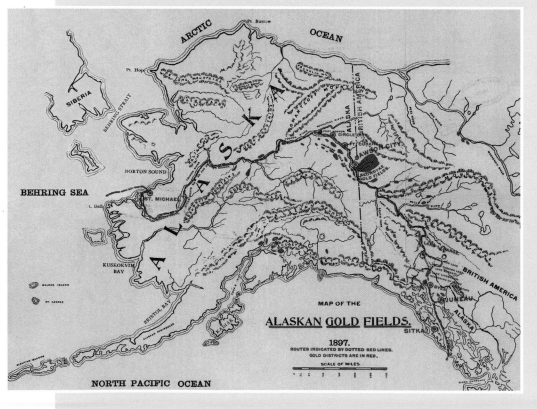

In July of 1897, ships arrived in Seattle and San Francisco carrying a few dozen happy prospectors and a lot of gold. Suddenly the outside world learned that gold had been discovered deep in the interior of Alaska and the Yukon, and thousands of people wanted to know how they, too, could cash in on the bonanza. Maps, such as this one, met the demand for information about a faraway place that most Americans had never even thought about, much less considered visiting.

A traditional dance in the Pacific Ocean island group of Samoa. This illustration is based on sketches and information gathered by the U.S. Exploring Expedition of 1838–1842. Led by Lieutenant Charles Wilkes of the U.S. Navy, the expedition visited many Pacific islands. The U.S. government later argued that these visits were a basis for considering some of these islands to be U.S. territory.

about the faraway northern wilderness that the great majority of them would never see. In the end, Alaska produced less gold than California or Canada's neighboring Yukon Territory, but seal hunting, whaling, and fishing industries became Alaska's major businesses. Most of all, though, Americans were simply proud to have added a place twice as large as Texas to their nation's territory. The expansionists, those who longed to see the United States grow into an American empire, felt that Alaska was a step in the right direction.

Pacific Territories

"The Pacific is our ocean," declared Albert Beveridge, a U.S. senator from Indiana in 1900.

For years, many Americans had shared his view that the United States should be the dominant power in the Pacific and the countries that bordered it. Secretary of State Seward was an early believer in the importance of the Pacific. Usually remembered for buying Alaska, Seward also acquired Midway, a pair of small islands in the middle of the ocean, where ships bound for China could refuel. He also had his eye on Hawaii, a much larger and more fertile island group.

Hawaii was an independent kingdom ruled by its own royal family. Beginning around 1800, however, foreign traders began to gain influence in the islands. American influence grew very quickly after the 1820s, when **missionaries**

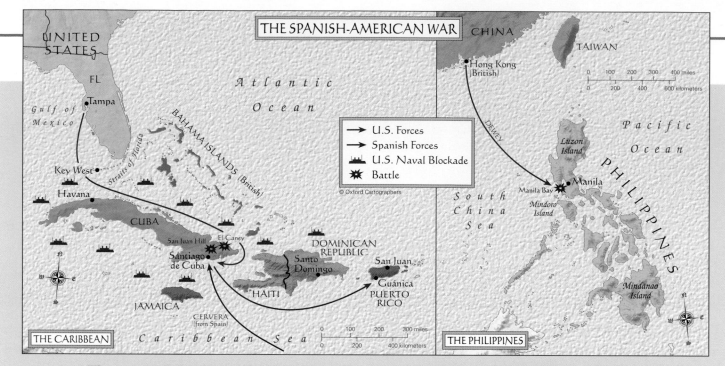

The roots of the Spanish-American War were in Cuba, in the Caribbean Sea, but the conflict stretched halfway around the world, to the Philippine Islands, in the western Pacific. The war began as a Cuban fight for independence from Spain. The United States got involved when the fight hurt American businesses and investments in Cuba, especially U.S.-owned sugar plantations and mills. U.S. forces fought and overwhelmed Spanish ones, not only in Cuba, but in Spain's other colony, the Philippines.

One hero of the war was Commodore George Dewey, who commanded part of the U.S. Navy's Pacific fleet. He steamed into Manila Bay in the Philippines and destroyed the Spanish fleet there, with only seven of his men slightly injured in the battle.

from the United States established settlements, schools, churches, and sugarcane plantations in Hawaii. American planters and landowners in Hawaii grew increasingly powerful in local politics and economic matters, and in 1887, the United States forced the king of Hawaii to allow the U.S. to build a naval base at the port called Pearl Harbor. But when Queen Liliuokalani came to the Hawaiian throne in 1891, she decided that Hawaiians should regain some control of their islands. The white planters in the islands responded by overthrowing her and setting up their own government. This gave the United States an excuse to **annex** Hawaii in 1898. Two years later, Hawaii officially became a U.S. territory. Samoa, an island group between the United States and Australia, suffered a similar fate, although the United States split the Samoa Islands with Germany.

The Spanish-American War

America's boldest role in international affairs began with a mysterious explosion and ended with the United States in control of territory in the Caribbean Sea and on the edge of Asia. The Caribbean islands of Cuba and Puerto Rico were among Spain's first colonies in the Americas, and until the 1890s, they remained under Spanish rule. When the Cuban people launched a revolt against the Spanish, many Americans wanted the United States to help them. Some Americans felt genuine sympathy for the Cubans who sought independence, but others simply wanted to protect U.S. businesses in Cuba and to have the island under United States control.

The United States sent the warship *Maine* to Havana, Cuba, to keep an eye on things, but America stayed out of the conflict. Then, in February 1898, a tremendous explosion destroyed the *Maine*, killing some 260 on board. The blast is now thought to have been caused by an accidental explosion in the ship's own engines, but war-minded Americans were sure that it was a sneak attack by the Spanish. In April, the United States declared war on Spain. The Spanish-American War was fought

The Spanish-American War was a great success for New Yorker Theodore Roosevelt, commander of a group of mounted volunteer soldiers nicknamed the Rough Riders. In Cuba in 1898, Roosevelt led the Rough Riders to victory at the Battle of San Juan Hill, earning fame that would help him win the U.S. presidency three years later.

in both the Caribbean and the Pacific, where Spain claimed the enormous island chain called the Philippines as its territory. In both places, U.S. forces managed to destroy most of the Spanish naval fleet and overcome its ground troops. Spain signed a peace **treaty** in August. Under the treaty, the United States took control of Puerto Rico, the Philippines, and the Pacific island of Guam, another

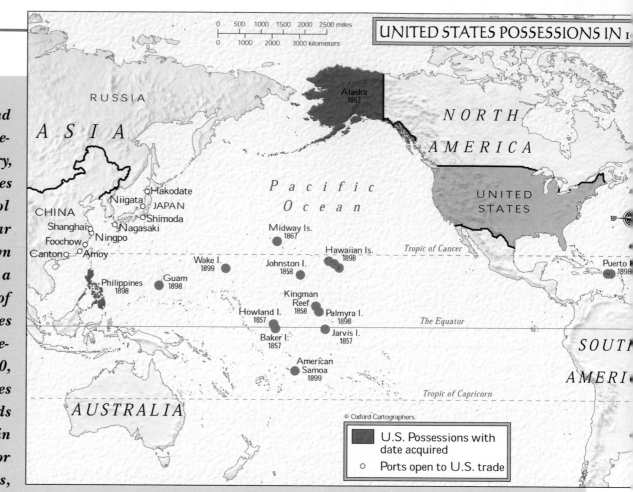

During the second half of the nineteenth century, the United States gained control of territory far beyond its own borders through a combination of peaceful treaties and war settlements. By 1900, the United States controlled islands that had been in Spanish hands for hundreds of years, from Puerto Rico in the Caribbean to the Philippines on the edge of Asia. Ports in China and Japan had also agreed to accept U.S. trade ships—often under the threat of force from America's superior navy. In its strength, and in the broad reach of its influence, America had become a world power.

Spanish territory. Cuba became officially independent, but the United States was recognized as having special interests and powers in the island, which was really under U.S. rule. The war was a victory for Senator Beveridge and others who wanted America to be an empire, not just a nation.

Across Panama

One barrier to world trade was the long and dangerous sea route around the tip of South America. The stormy waters there linked the Atlantic and Pacific Oceans, but they added weeks and thousands of miles to shipping routes. As early as the 1600s, the Spanish con-

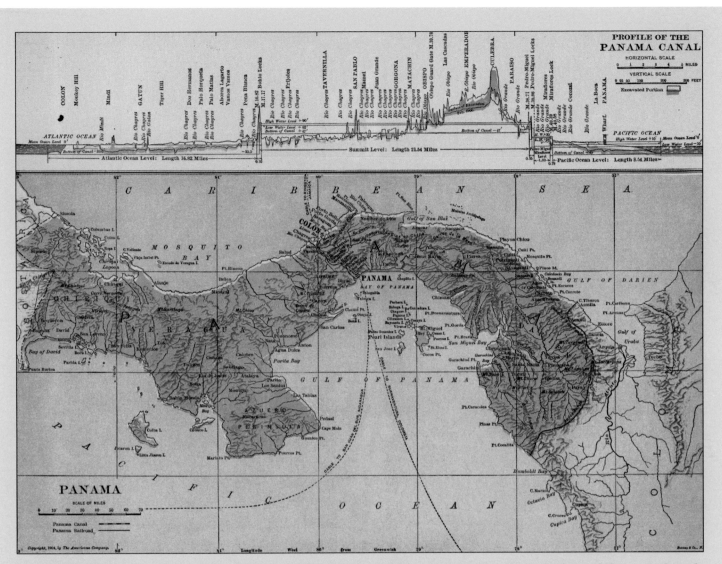

Published ten years before the Panama Canal opened, this map shows the location of the canal and gives an idea of the challenges faced by its engineers and laborers. The top portion of the map is a profile, or side view, of the Isthmus of Panama, the neck of land that the canal crosses. It reveals the height and steepness of the hills through which workers had to cut, and it also shows the various levels of the canal, which would be linked by locks. Newspaper articles and maps such as this one helped keep the American public interested in the canal project and willing to support it.

Workers armed with picks (left) and shovels dig through a landslide blocking a narrow part of the Panama Canal known as the Gaillard or Culebra Cut. Less than a year later, in August 1914, ships pass through the Cut (right) on their way from one ocean to another. The Panama Canal was the biggest change that humans had ever made to the geography of the world, and Americans proudly regarded it as a triumph of their national skill and determination.

querors of Central America had dreamed of cutting a canal through a narrow part of the Americas to link the two oceans. By the late nineteenth century, the French—successful builders of the Suez Canal between the Mediterranean and Red Seas—were ready to try digging such a canal through Panama. High costs and the sheer difficulty of working in jungles and swamps filled with mosquitoes that carried the deadly diseases malaria and yellow fever were factors in their failure.

The United States decided to take over. Although Panama was part of the South American nation of Colombia, and Colombia turned down the U.S. offer for the land, Americans didn't take no for an answer. A revolt against Colombian rule was just starting in Panama, so the United States sent a warship to Panama to encourage the rebellion and promptly recognized Panama's independence. In turn, Panama quickly signed a treaty giving the United States control of the Canal Zone, a strip of land crossing the country. Just as it had swept political difficulties out of its path, the United States dealt with practical problems. While an army doctor introduced successful measures to control the

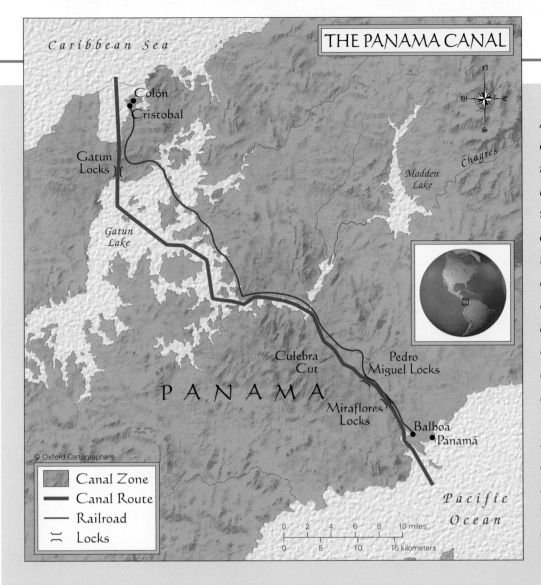

THE PANAMA CANAL

Built across one of the narrowest parts of Central America, the Panama Canal is fifty-one miles (eighty-two kilometers) long. Because the canal crosses hills, it would have been immensely difficult and costly to dig the entire route down to sea level. As a result, part of the canal is above sea level, and enormous chambers called locks are flooded or drained to raise or lower ships from one level to another. The United States controlled the Canal Zone, a strip of land on each side of the canal, until 1979, when it returned the territory to Panama. Twenty years later, the United States turned the canal itself over to Panama. The United States still has influence over the canal, however—a special treaty allows it to defend the canal if necessary.

mosquitoes, thousands of workers laid a railroad, dug and blasted channels, and built the canal's brilliantly designed locks, chambers that could be filled or drained to raise and lower ships from one level of the canal to another.

The Panama Canal opened for business in August 1914. Ships of all nations could use the canal, on payment of a fee, but the biggest benefit was to the United States. By cutting 7,000 miles from the sea journey between America's two coasts, the canal not only helped trade but let the U.S. Navy move more quickly than ever from one part of the world to another. America had won its place among the world powers—now many people wondered how it would use its strength.

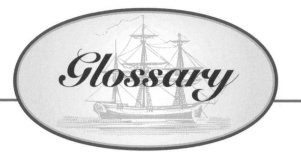

Glossary

annex: to enlarge a nation or state by adding territory that was formerly outside its borders

immigrant: one who enters a new country

immigration: arrival of foreigners into a country

missionary: someone who works to convert other people to his or her religion

ore: rock that contains a commercially significant amount of a mineral

refinery: plant for processing petroleum to preparc it for commercial use

reservation: area assigned to Native Americans by the U.S. government

rural: relating to the countryside or to country life

transcontinental: crossing an entire continent

treaty: formal agreement between peoples or nations

urban: relating to cities or city life

Map List

ABOUT THE HISTORICAL MAPS
The historical maps used in this book are primary source documents found in the Library of Congress Map Division. You will find these maps on pages: 12, 17, 30, 31, 36, 41.

Chronology

1861   Telegraph wires link the East and West Coasts of the United States.

1862   The Homestead Act launches the settlement of the Great Plains.

1865   The Civil War ends.

1867   The United States buys Alaska from Russia.

1869   The first transcontinental railroad line links the eastern and western United States.

1876   Alexander Graham Bell invents the telephone.

1879   Thomas Alva Edison invents the incandescent light bulb.

1884   The country's first skyscraper, a ten-story building, is built in Chicago.

1886   The Statue of Liberty is placed on an island in New York Harbor.

1889   Homesteaders flock to one of the last unsettled territories in the Oklahoma land rush.

1890   Congress tries to limit the power of big business with the Sherman Antitrust Act.

1898   The United States fights Spain in Cuba and the Philippines during the Spanish-American War.

1900   Hawaii becomes a U.S. territory.

1903   The Wright brothers make the first successful airplane flight.

1908   Henry Ford begins mass producing the Model T automobile.

1914   The U.S.-built Panama Canal opens, linking the Atlantic and Pacific Oceans.

Further Reading

Gaines, Ann. *The Panama Canal in American History.*
Springfield, NJ: Enslow Publishers, 1999.

Katz, William Loren. *The Great Migrations, 1880s–1912.*
Austin, TX: Raintree Steck-Vaughn, 1993.

Marrin, Albert. *The Spanish-American War.* New York:
Atheneum, 1991.

McCormick, Anita L. *The Industrial Revolution in American History.* Springfield, NJ: Enslow Publishers, 1998.

Murphy, Jim. *Across America on an Emigrant Train.*
New York: Clarion Books, 1993.

Stein, R. Conrad. *The Transcontinental Railroad in American History.* Springfield, NJ: Enslow Publishers, 1997.

Takaki, Ronald, adapted by Rebecca Stefoff.
Spacious Dreams: The First Wave of Asian Immigration. New York: Chelsea House, 1994.

WEBSITES

The Center for Immigration Studies
www.cis.org

The University of Minnesota's Immigration
History Resource Center
www.umn.edu/ihrc/

The New York Public Library
www.nypl.org/research/chss/epo/spanexhib/
A War in Perspective. 1898–1998. Public Appeals,
Memory, and the Spanish-American Conflict.

Discovery Online
www.discovery.com/stories/history/panama/panama/html

ABOUT THE AUTHOR

Rebecca Stefoff is the author of Marshall Cavendish's
North American Historical Atlases series and many
other nonfiction books for children and young adults.
Her special interests include the settling of the West,
geography, and military history. She now makes her
home in Portland, Oregon.

Index

Entries are filed letter-by-letter. Page numbers for illustrations and maps are in **boldface**.